# 120
# Audubon
# BIRD PRINTS

## CD-ROM & BOOK

John James Audubon

Dover Publications, Inc.
Mineola, New York

The CD-ROM in this book contains all of the images. There is no installation necessary. Just insert the CD into your computer and call the images into your favorite software (refer to the documentation with your software for further instructions). Each image has been scanned at 300 dpi and saved in both 72-dpi Internet-ready and 300-dpi high-resolution JPEG format.

The "Images" folder on the CD contains two different folders. All of the high-resolution JPEG files have been placed in one folder and all of the Internet-ready JPEG files can be found in the other folder. The images in each of these folders are identical. Every image has a unique file name in the following format: xxx.JPG. The first 3 digits of the file name, before the period, correspond to the number printed under the image in the book. The last 3 letters of the file name "JPG," refer to the file format. So, 001.JPG would be the first file in the JPEG folder.

Also included on the CD-ROM is Dover Design Manager, a simple graphics editing program for Windows that will allow you to view, print, crop, and rotate the images.

For technical support, contact:
Telephone: 1 (617) 249-0245
Fax: 1 (617) 249-0245
Email: dover@artimaging.com
Internet: **http://www.dovertechsupport.com**
The fastest way to receive technical support is via email or the Internet.

*Bibliographical Note*

*120 Audubon Bird Prints CD-ROM and Book,* first published by Dover Publications, Inc., in 2008, is a new selection of plates from the octavo edition of *The Birds of America, from Drawings Made in the United States and Their Territories,* by John James Audubon, F. R. SS. L. & E., first published in New York by J. J. Audubon and in Philadephia by J. B. Chevalier from 1840 through 1844.

## Dover Electronic Clip Art®

*International Standard Book Number*
*ISBN-13: 978-0-486-99854-1*
*ISBN-10: 0-486-99854-1*

Manufactured in the United States of America
Dover Publications, Inc., 31 East 2nd Street, Mineola, N.Y. 11501

002. White-winged Crossbill; males *(red)*, females *(yellow)*.

001. Evening Grosbeak; male *(top)*, young male *(middle)*, female *(bottom)*.

**004.** Purple Finch; males *(red)*, female *(brown)*.

**003.** American Goldfinch; male *(top)*, female *(bottom)*.

**006.** Summer Tanager; male (*top*), female (*middle*), young male (*bottom*).

**005.** Common Redpoll; male (*top*), female (*bottom*).

008. Western Tanager; males *(top, middle)*, female *(bottom)*.

007. Scarlet Tanager; male *(top)*, female *(bottom)*.

**010.** Troupial, male.

**009.** Northern Oriole; adult male *(top)*, young male *(middle)*, female *(bottom)*.

**012.** Common Grackle; female *(top)*, male *(bottom)*.

**011.** Orchard Oriole; adult male *(top)*, young male *(middle)*, female *(bottom)*.

**014.** Red-winged Blackbird; adult male *(top)*, young male *(bottom left)*, female *(bottom right)*.

**013.** Yellow-headed Blackbird; female *(top)*, male *(bottom left)*, young male *(bottom right)*.

**016.** Bobolink; male *(top)*, female *(bottom)*.

**015.** Eastern Meadowlark; males *(top, bottom left)*, females *(bottom right, in nest)*.

**018.** Dickcissel; male *(top)*, female *(bottom)*.

**017.** Snow Bunting; adults *(top, middle)*, young *(bottom)*.

**020.** Dark-eyed Junco; female *(top)*, male *(bottom)*.

**019.** White-throated Sparrow; female *(top)*, male *(bottom)*.

**022.** Painted Bunting; female *(top)*, males in different states of plumage *(bottom three)*.

**021.** Rufous-sided Towhee; male *(top)*, female *(bottom)*.

**024.** Blue Grosbeak; male *(top)*, young *(middle)*, female *(bottom)*.

**023.** Indigo Bunting; males in different states of plumage *(top three)*, female *(bottom)*.

**026.** Rose-breasted Grosbeak; young male *(top)*, female *(middle)*, males *(bottom two)*.

**025.** Northern Cardinal; male *(top)*, female *(bottom)*.

**028.** Common Yellowthroat; young male *(top)*, adult male *(middle)*, female *(bottom)*.

**027.** Black-headed Grosbeak: males *(top, bottom right)*, female *(bottom left)*.

030. Canada Warbler, male.

029. Yellow-breasted Chat; males *(top three)*, female *(in nest)*.

**032.** Bay-breasted Warbler; male *(top)*, female *(bottom)*.

**031.** Yellow Warbler, males.

**034.** Chestnut-sided Warbler; female (*top*), male (*bottom*).

**033.** Magnolia Warbler; young (*top*), male (*middle*), female (*bottom*).

**036.** Black-throated Blue Warbler; male *(top)*, female *(bottom)*.

**035.** Cerulean Warbler; old male *(top)*, young male *(bottom)*.

**038.** Blue-winged Warbler; male *(top)*, female *(bottom)*.

**037.** Northern Parula; male *(top)*, female *(bottom)*.

**040.** Warbling Vireo; male *(top)*, female *(bottom)*.

**039.** Prothonotary Warbler; male *(top)*, female *(bottom)*.

**042.** Northern Mockingbird; males *(top, middle)*, female *(bottom)*.

**041.** Cedar Waxwing; female *(top)*, male *(bottom)*.

**044.** Loggerhead Shrike; female *(left)*, male *(right)*.

**043.** Gray Catbird; male *(top)*, female *(bottom)*.

**046.** Veery, male.

**045.** American Robin; male *(top left)*, female *(top right)*, young *(bottom five)*.

**048.** Western Bluebird; male *(top)*, female *(bottom)*.

**047.** Eastern Bluebird; male *(top)*, female *(middle)*, young *(bottom)*.

**050.** Blue-gray Gnatcatcher; male *(top)*, female *(bottom)*.

**049.** Wood Thrush; male *(top)*, female *(bottom)*.

**052.** White-breasted Nuthatch; females *(top, bottom)*, male *(middle)*.

**051.** Ruby-crowned Kinglet; male *(top)*, female *(bottom)*.

**054.** Tufted Titmouse; male (*top*), female (*bottom*).

**053.** Brown Creeper; female (*top*), male (*bottom*).

056. Common Raven, old male.

055. Black-capped Chickadee; male *(top)*, female *(bottom)*.

058. Magpie Jay, males.

057. American Crow, male.

**060.** Purple Martin.

**059.** Blue Jay; females *(top, bottom left)*, male *(bottom right)*.

**061.** Horned Lark, male.

**062.** Pileated Woodpecker; adult female *(top)*, adult male *(middle)*, young males *(bottom two)*.

**064.** Downy Woodpecker; male *(top)*, female *(bottom)*.

**063.** Hairy Woodpecker; female *(top)*, male *(bottom)*.

**066.** Belted Kingfisher; males (*top, middle*), female (*bottom*).

**065.** Northern Flicker; female (*top*), male (*bottom*).

**068.** Anna's Hummingbird; males *(top two)*, female *(bottom)*.

**067.** Ruby-throated Hummingbird; males *(top left, middle)*, female *(top right)*, young *(bottom)*.

**070.** Eastern Screech Owl.

**069.** Whip-poor-will.

072. Great Gray Owl.

071. Snowy Owl.

**074.** Carolina Parakeet; males *(top, middle)*, female *(bottom left)*, young *(bottom right)*.

**073.** Great Horned Owl.

**076.** Passenger Pigeon; female *(top)*, male *(bottom)*.

**075.** Mourning Dove; males *(top right, middle)*, females *(top left, bottom)*.

077. Wild Turkey, male.

**078.** Mountain Quail; male *(left)*, female *(right)*.

080. Osprey.

079. Gyrfalcon.

082. California Condor.

081. Red-shouldered Hawk.

**083.** Black Vulture.

**084.** Bald Eagle.

**085.** Great Auk, adult.

**086.** Atlantic Puffin; female *(in nest)*, male *(standing)*.

**087.** Royal Tern, male.

**088.** Red-necked Phalarope; female *(top)*, male *(bottom left)*, young in autumn *(bottom right)*.

**090.** Herring Gull; adult in spring (*top*), young in autumn (*bottom*).

**089.** Great Black-backed Gull, male.

**091.** Upland Sandpiper; female *(top)*, male *(bottom)*.

**092.** Red Knot; summer plumage *(left)*, winter plumage *(right)*.

**093.** American Woodcock; female *(top)*, young in autumn *(bottom left)*, male *(bottom right)*.

**094.** Long-billed Curlew.

**095.** Piping Plover; female *(left)*, male *(right)*.

**096.** Black-necked Stilt, male.

**097.** American Avocet; young in first winter plumage *(front),* adult *(back).*

**098.** American Oystercatcher, male.

**099.** Black Oystercatcher, female.

**100.** Clapper Rail; female *(left)*, male *(right)*.

**101.** Common Merganser; female *(left)*, male *(right)*.

**102.** Common Goldeneye; male *(left)*, female *(right)*.

**103.** Northern Shoveler; male *(left)*, female *(right)*.

**104.** American Wigeon; male *(top)*, female *(bottom)*.

**105.** Mallard; males *(green heads)*, females *(brown heads)*.

**106.** Wood Duck; males *(left top and bottom)*, females *(right top and bottom)*.

108. Whooping Crane, adult male.

107. Canada Goose; male (*standing*), female (*sitting*).

**110.** Tundra Swan, male.

**111.** Roseate Spoonbill, male.

**112.** Glossy Ibis, adult male.

**113.** Tricolored Heron, adult male.

**114.** Great Blue Heron, male.

116. Wood Stork, male.

115. Snowy Egret, male.

118. American White Pelican, male.

117. Double-crested Cormorant, male.

**119.** Light–mantled Sooty Albatross.

**120.** Common Loon; young in winter *(left)*, adult *(right)*.

# INDEX